# SCHIRMER'S LIBRARY OF MUSICAL CLASSICS

SONATA ALBUM

Twenty-Six Favorite Sonatas

For the Piano

By

HAYDN, MOZART, and BEETHOVEN

Edited, Revised, and Fingered by

SIGMUND LEBERT, HANS von BÜLOW
AND OTHERS

IN TWO BOOKS

Book I: 15 SONATAS — Library Volume 329

⟶ Book II: 11 SONATAS — Library Volume 340

G. SCHIRMER, Inc.

DISTRIBUTED BY

HAL•LEONARD
CORPORATION

7777 W. BLUEMOUND RD. P.O. BOX 13819 MILWAUKEE, WI 53213

Contents

Book I

Haydn

Mozart

Beethoven

Contents
Book II

Haydn

16.  Allegretto innocente. *mp*

17.  Allegro. *mf*

18.  Allegro moderato. *f*

Mozart

19.  Allegro assai. *f*

21.  Allegro. *p*

20.  Allegro. *mf*

22.  Allegro maestoso. *f*

Beethoven

23.  Grave. *f* *p* *f* *p*

25.  Adagio sostenuto.

24.  Allegro. *p*

26.  Andante con Variazioni. *p*

SONATA.

Abbreviations: M. T. signifies Main Theme; Ep., Episode; S. T., Sub-Theme; Cl. T., Closing Theme; D. G.,
Development-Group; Md. T., Mid-Theme; R., Return; Tr., Transition; Cod., Codetta; I, II, and III, 1st, 2nd,
and 3rd parts of a movement in song-form (Liedform.)

JOSEPH HAYDN.

Allegretto innocente. (♩= 72.)

a) ... easier: ...   b) ... easier: ...   c) After the hold lift both hands together,
and continue after a brief pause.   d) ... easier: ...

2

Printed in the U. S. A.

a) As at c) on preceding page.

3

a) Sustain long, and proceed only after a prolonged pause: b) ♪♪♪♪♪♪ easier: ♪♪♪♪♪

5

a) ♪♪♪♪♪♪ b) ♪♪♪♪♪♪

SONATA.

Abbreviations: M. T. signifies Main Theme; Ep., Episode; S. T., Sub-Theme; Cl. T., Closing Theme; D. G., Development-group; Md. T., Mid-Theme; R., Return; Tr., Transition; Cod., Codetta; I, II, and III, signify 1st, 2nd, and 3rd parts of a movement in song-form (Lied-form).

JOSEPH HAYDN.

a) Make a considerable pause after the hold itself.
b) This accompaniment-figure in the left hand must be subordinated to the right-hand part throughout.

Printed in the U.S.A.

c) Both hands must begin and end the *arpeggio* together, and with a *crescendo* in the right-hand part, so that its highest tone may be the most prominent.

a) As at b) on 1st Page of this Sonata.

b) Begin the embellishment together with the first bass note.

a) After lifting both hands, proceed instantly.
b) Make a considerable pause after this hold.

a) As at b), on 1st page of this Sonata.

a) As at c), on Page 29.

a) Throughout the movement the melody must be made duly prominent, but without any harshness.

b) The execution of these 2 measures is like that of the first 2. In all cases, embellishments take their time-value from that of the principal note with which they are connected by a slur, as the above example shows.

14

a) This grace is also played as a short turn in 4 equal notes, falling on the sixth 16th-note of the accompaniment-figure.
b) The 3 **grace**-notes coincide, as a triplet, with the third 16th-note of the accompaniment-figure.

Finale.

Tempo di Menuetto. ($\flat$ = 126.)

*) The time-value of this grace is taken from that of the preceding eighth-rest, as follows:

a)

18

SONATA.

Abbreviations: M.T. signifies Main Theme; Ep., Episode; S.T., Sub-Theme; Cl. T., Closing Theme; D.G., Development-group; Md. T., Mid-Theme; R., Return; Tr., Transition; Cod., Codetta; I, II, III, 1st, 2nd, and 3rd parts of a movement in song-form (Liedform).

Revised and Fingered by
LUDWIG KLEE.

JOSEPH HAYDN.

27

Sonata II
(K. No. 280)

Edited, revised and fingered by
Richard Epstein

Abbreviations: P.T., Principal Theme; S.T., Secondary Theme; M.T., Middle Theme; D., Development.

Abreviaciones: T. P., Tema Principal; T. S., Tema Segundo; T. M., Tema Medio; D., Desarrollo.

Allegro assai (♩ = 138)

P.T.
T.P.

Close
Coda

a)

a) The lower notes F, D, F, D may be played with the left hand.

a) Las notas inferiores Fa, Re, Fa, Re pueden tocarse con la mano izquierda.

a) Like a) preceding page.

a) Como a) de la página precedente.

41

Sonata VII
(K. No. 333)

Edited, revised and fingered by
Richard Epstein

Abbreviations: P. T., Principal Theme; S. T., Secondary Theme; D., Development; Ep., Episode; R., Return.

Abreviaciones: T. P., Tema Principal; T. S., Tema Segundo; D., Desarrollo; Ep., Episodio; R., Retorno.

Close I
1ª Coda

Allegretto grazioso (♩= 138)

59

Sonata IV

(K. No. 533)

Edited, revised and fingered by
Richard Epstein

Abbreviations: P.T., Principal Theme; S.T., Secondary Theme; Ep., Episode; T., Transition; D., Development.

Abreviaciones: T.P., Tema Principal; T.S., Tema
Segundo; Ep., Episodio; T., Transición; D., Desarrollo.

W. A. MOZART

Close
Coda

Maggiore

Coda. Anh.

a)

ritard. e dim.

a)

82

Sonata XIV
(K. No. 310)

Edited, revised and fingered by
Richard Epstein

Abbreviations: P.T., Principal Theme; S.T., Secondary Theme; D., Development; Ep., Episode; M.T., Middle Theme; R., Return.

Abreviaciones: T. P., Tema Principal; T. S., Tema Segundo; D., Desarrollo; Ep., Episodio; T. M., Tema Medio; R., Retorno.

Printed in the U.S.A.

marcato

calando   p

Ped.   *

f

p

Ped.   *   Ped.   *   Ped.   *   Ped.   *

S.T.
T.S.

p

p

Andante cantabile con espressione (♩=96)

90

92

100

SONATE PATHÉTIQUE.

Op. 13.

To Prince CARL von LICHNOWSKY.

Abbreviations: M.T. signifies Main Theme; S.T., Sub-Theme; Cl.T., Closing Theme; D.G., Development-group; R., Return; Tr., Transition; Md.T., Mid-Theme; Ep., Episode.

Grave. (♪ = 66.)

L. van BEETHOVEN.

a) The 32nd-note must be perceptibly detached from the next-following dotted sixteenth-note, and this latter sustained for its full value — a mode of execution peculiar to such rhythms in the old masters; compare Händel's Prelude to the F-minor Fugue, and Bach's Prelude to the G-minor Fugue in Part II of "The Well-tempered Clavichord."

b) This run should be performed expressively, and in the second half with a slight retardation, so as to bring out the melodic outlines.

c) Carefully observe the increasing value of the "lifting-note;" the first time, the sixth eighth in the measure is only a sixteenth-note; in the next measure, the D on the second eighth is a full eighth-note, while the F on the sixth eighth becomes a quarter-note. This effects a melodic intensification.

Copyright, 1894, by G. Schirmer, Inc. Printed in the U.S.A. *Copyright renewal assigned, 1923, to G. Schirmer, Inc.*

a) The relation between the movement of the *Introduction* and the *Allegro* is properly this: That a whole note in the latter is exactly equivalent to an eighth-note in the former. Consequently, the *Allegro* may be begun at the rate of M.M. ♩=132, which movement would not, however, be fast enough further on, in view of the passionate character developed.

b) In tremolo-figures like these, the player should be content to mark only such bass notes (and then only at the first stroke) as indicate a new progression in the harmony.

c) The direction *agitato* also calls for a *non legato* as strict as possible, which, of course, must not impair the e-venness of the movement.

a) Although this "*second*" subject, too, is passionately agitated, the unvarying tempestuous sweep of the first cannot be kept up throughout. Play the first measure of each four-measure period—the preluding bass—somewhat more quietly, the following three with all the more animation; shade the 16 measures in Eb-minor differently from the parallel passage in Db-major; in short, invest the entire dialogue with the most varied coloring possible.

b) Execution: according to the familiar rule, that all graces take their value from, and are played within, the value of the principal note.

c) Execution: according to the same rule; beware of the facile and tasteless triplet in eighth-notes, to which even the anticipated passing shake would be preferable, though against the rules.

a) These first 4 measures are to be played without the least retardation, yet very quietly, and with no accentuation of the accompaniment.

a) The hold (pause) must be sustained precisely 3 measures, so as to form another 4-measure period.

But a quarter-rest should precede the reprise of the first division:

b) Retard the entrance of the B in the bass, in order to enhance the pleasurable suspense attendant upon the enharmonic change of the diminished chord of the seventh in the transition from G-minor to E-minor; and play the following passage throughout with full dreamy freedom.

a) Despite the identity of this phrase with that in meas. 5 of the first *Grave*, it must now be played with a wholly different expression——or, rather, with none whatever, this being rendered necessary by the doubled rapidity of the movement (♩ in the *Grave* = ○ in the *Allegro*).

b) Although the phrasing 𝄞 etc. would more nearly correspond to the original form of this passage in meas. 7 *et seq.* of the so-called second subject (E♭-minor), it would not be in keeping with the general (progressional) character of the development-section.

c) The player should slightly sustain the several tones 𝄞 but not so as to make the movement heavy.

107

a) As an exception to the rule, this trill must not begin on the auxiliary, so as not to blur the melodic

outlines: seven notes vigorously played suffice in such rapid tempo.

a) This *piano* must enter abruptly, which requires some practice, especially with the left hand; similarly in the parallel passage 4 measures further on.

a) In the original the *decrescendo* begins at this measure, which seems to us rather too prolonged for 6 full measures, — the more so, because an actual *forte* would be inadmissible in the preceding; for this reason we consider a *poco cresc.* more suitable for the first two measures.

b) Take care not to play E♭ instead of F in the right hand, as a C-minor chord is out of the question here; the C in both Soprano and Bass is simply a passing-note of the dominant chord.

Coda.

Grave.

Allegro molto e con brio.

a) Sustain the hold (pause) 3 full measures (comp. {Note a, the first holds in the *Grave* have precisely the same dura-
tion (subtracting the 32nd-note). Page 112);

b) The bass note on the third fourth-note must have a penetrating and prolonged tone, in order to be quite audible
through the seventh eighth-note as the root of the chord of the sixth.

c) This coda cannot be played too rapidly.

d) It is best not to use the pedal with these chords.

Adagio cantabile. ($\bullet$= 60)

a) To the best of our knowledge no one has yet remarked the striking affinity of the theme of this movement, even with reference to its external melodic structure, to that of one of the loftiest *Adagios* of grandest scope from the Master's last period;— we mean the *Adagio* of the Ninth Symphony, written almost a quarter of a century later. The performance of both demands an equally inspired mood. The player's task, to "make his fingers sing," may perhaps necessitate a more frequent use of the pedal than we have indicated, which must of course be controlled by a most watchful ear.

b) This first middle section of the Rondo (for such this *Adagio* is in form) may be taken slightly *meno andante*, i. e., slower; but no more so than needful (so as not to drag), and therefore, in only a few places.

c) The turns in this and the next measure should not commence with, but immediately after, a sixteenth-note in the bass,

a) A tasteful execution of this grace is impossible in strict time. An abbreviation of the first two principal notes (C and B♭) being quite as impracticable as a shifting of the inverted mordent into the preceding measure as an unaccented appoggiatura, the measure must simply be extended by an additional 32nd-note.

b) In this repetition of the theme, the left hand may be allowed to play a more expressive part; and, on the whole, a somewhat lighter shading of the melody is now admissible by way of contrast to the following (gloomier) middle section.

c) The ascending diminished fifth may be phrased, as it were, like a question, to which the succeeding bass figure may be regarded as the answer.

a) It appears advisable slightly to hasten this measure and the next, and then to retard the third not inconsiderably; the former on account of the cessation in the harmonic advance, the latter by reason of the varied modulation, which must be quite free from disquieting haste in its return to the theme.

b) Though strictly subordinated to the melody, the triplets should be brought out with animated distinctness.

c) The two 32nd-notes in the melody may very properly be sounded with the last note of the triplet of 16th-notes in the accompaniment; whereas a mathematically exact division would probably confuse both parts.

a) Execute like a triplet:

b) In the original, the shading of this passage is marked differently from that two measures before, the *diminuendo* already beginning with C, and not with A♭ as here marked. This latter nuance — the prolongation of the *crescendo* — appeals to our feeling as the more delicate, "more tenderly passionate," to quote Richard Wagner's happy remark on the "Interpretation of Beethoven."

c) Mark the separation of the slurs in this figure and those following; the six notes sound trivial if slurred together.

Rondo.

Allegro. (♩=96.)

a) Although this third movement is less "pathetic" than the preceding ones, the player alone will be to blame should the Pathetic Sonata end apathetically. The original, to be sure, contains only the most indispensable expression-marks, which it has been the aim of our Edition to supplement efficiently; as, for example, by the *crescendo* ending *piano* in measures 2-3, by emphasizing the distinction to be made, in the figures for the left hand, between the parts (tones) which are essential (independent) organic elements, and those which are mere harmonic filling; etc.

b) In executing this grace, the player must be careful not to produce the effect of parallel octaves with the bass (F-A♭, and in the next measure E♭-G); rather than this, the slide might be treated as an appendage to the foregoing notes.

a) There can hardly be a doubt that the Master was compelled, by the restricted compass of the keyboard of his day (only up to F³), to content himself with the fifth of the dominant chord, instead of rising to the higher seventh (A♭) as in the three other parallel passages. A change in conformity with his original intention is impracticable, however, because the ensuing measure would then be made to lie an octave higher, and would sound somewhat thin for the first time (it is immediately repeated in the octave).

b) These imitations, although *piano,* must be played with great animation, and not in that characterless *legato* which might be called anti-symphonic.

c) The preceding Remark applies equally to this and similar passages.

a) The fingering given by us serves to aid in executing this run with the exact rhythmic divisions desired by the composer. The hold which follows appears really superfluous; for, by the prolongation of the chord through $1\frac{4}{4}$ measures, all demands of the pulsing rhythm ___ which goes on even during the rests of a piece ___ are fully met.

Tranquillo. a)

a) The tempo, of course, remains the same, but free from any fluctuating agitation. Observe, that the theme "proper" begins with an ascending fourth, consequently, the left hand should be slightly emphasized in the fifth and sixth measures. This holds good for meas. 13, 14, etc.

b) The mark *ff* is set rather early, in view of the fact, that the intensification continues through the next six measures. For this reason, the player will do well to husband his strength at first.

a) The more tempestuously the 12 preceding measures have been played, the longer may this hold (see Note a, page 154) be sustained.

12589

a) The second subject must be played more delicately and quietly here than at its first entrance in E♭ major.

b) A collision of the two parts on D² must be avoided by anticipating the right hand by an arpeggio in the left, lifting the left-hand thumb instantly after the stroke; thus:

c) The second note in the bass might, in conformity with the parallel passages in the first division, be A♭.

12589

a) These next 13 measures should be played with considerable freedom as regards tempo, and with a decided independent stress on the lower part in the left hand. Special attention should be paid to the composer's directions concerning both the shading of meas. 6-7 and 8-9, and their phrasing, which is not in one-measure rhythm (as the motive at the first glance apparently invites), but in two-measure rhythm. In proportion to the greater or lesser degree of passion put forth by the player before the *calando,* this latter is to be conceived as a *diminuendo* and *ritardando.* Excess in either direction is, of course, reprehensible.

b) Particularly note the *Auftakt* (fractional initial measure) in the bass, here representing the regular introduction By playing the theme wholly without shading on its fourth (and last) appearance, the close is well prepared and led up to.

a) Moderate the tempo on commencing this measure, in order that the ensuing run can be executed precisely according to the given divisions and without the least retardation. The following hold may be sustained very long—as long as the sonority of the piano permits.

b) A *ritardando* in this epilogue would be in bad taste; the tempo must be strictly sustained to the close.

c) The *fff* is found in all the old Editions,—almost the sole instance where this superlative, surely as frequently intended as rarely used is employed by the Master. Hence follows the necessity of an unusually powerful *crescendo* in the preceding run.

SONATA.
Op. 2, № 1.

To JOSEPH HAYDN.

Abbreviations: *) M.T. signifies Main Theme; S.T., Sub-Theme; Cl.T., Closing Theme; D. G., Development-group; R., Return; Tr., Transition; Md. T., Mid-Theme; Ep., Episode.

L. van BEETHOVEN.

12589

a) easier:

Adagio. ($\downarrow$ = 88.)

a) 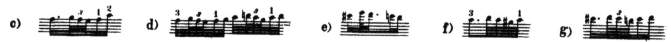   b) The left-hand part kept subordinate, though the sustained bass notes, in contrast to the 16ths, should be somewhat emphasized.

c)   d)   e)   f)   g)

Menuetto.
Allegretto. ($\dot{}$ = 63.)

Men. D. C.

a) In this theme *Piano* and *Forte* are to be sharply contradistinguished, without gradual transition from one to the other.

b)    c)

 136

a) In this accompaniment the left hand must be subordinated to the melody.

138

a)

a) The left hand, having the mélody, must play somewhat louder than the right, both here and on the repetition.

Sonata quasi una Fantasia.

To Countess JULIA GUICCIARDI.

Op. 27, Nº 2.

Abbreviations: M. T. signifies Main Theme; S. T., Sub-Theme; Cl. T., Closing Theme; D. G., Development-group; R., Return; Tr., Transition; Md. T., Mid-Theme; Ep., Episode.

I. Adagio sostenuto. (♩ = 52.)

L. van BEETHOVEN.

a) It is evident that the highest part, as the melody, requires a firmer touch than the accompanying triplet-figure; and the first note in the latter must never produce the effect of a doubling of the melody in the lower octave.

b) A more frequent use of the pedal than is marked by the editor, and limited here to the most essential passages, is allowable; it is not advisable, however, to take the original directions *sempre senza sordini* (i. e., without dampers) too literally.

143

a) The player must guard against carrying his hand back with over-anxious haste. For, in any event, a strict pedantic observance of time is out of place in this period, which has rather the character of an improvisation.

a) The notes with a dash above them may properly be dwelt upon in such a way as to give them the effect of suspensions, e. g., : in fact, a utilization of the inner parts, in accordance with the laws of euphony and the course of the modulation, is recommended throughout the piece.

II. Allegretto.a) (♩. = 56.)

a) *Allegretto* means *poco allegro*. The movement should not exceed a moderate minuet-tempo, in this point precisely resembling the analogous movements in the Sonatas Op. 2, Nᵒˢ 1 and 2; Op. 10, Nº 2; Op. 14, Nº 1, not to speak of later ones. This anti-Scherzo is, indeed, a lyrical Intermezzo between two tragical Nocturnes. Franz Liszt's clever *mot*: *"Une fleur entre deux abîmes"* (a flower betwixt two abysses) gives the key to the true interpretation.

b) Special care must be bestowed on the twofold task of the right hand — a songful leading of the melody, with a light and graceful *staccato* in the second part, which latter combines with the left-hand part as a third factor.

a) A very common amateurish error. — which, we regret to say, is countenanced here and in other places by Herr Lebert's otherwise so meritorious edition — is the notion that a closer *legato* is obtainable, in descending octave-passages, by a change of fingers. Precisely the opposite effect is produced by the following manipulation: the higher part, the one most strongly affecting the ear, suffers a most sensible interruption. A slight muscular stretching of the palm of the hand, which is no harder to learn than shifting on a stringed instrument, will amply fulfil all requirements.

b) An undelayed attack (of the Finale) is quite as indispensable to the general effect as in the two reprises preceding.

III. Presto agitato. ($\bullet$=88.)

a) This passage, up to the abrupt stroke on the fourth beat in measure 2, must be played with almost ethereal lightness in the very smoothest *piano*. and (if only for the sake of distinctness) as little *legato* as is in any way compatible with the great rapidity of the movement.

b) The second stroke has only the significance of an echo, the repercussion of the first. In measure 8 it is different, owing to its leading over to new matter.

a) This grace is written out in conformity with its undeviating mode of execution. Avoid a repeated accentuation of the lowest bass note; an accent is needful only on its first entrance.
b) The rapid movement, conjoined with required exertion of strength, hardly admits of a longer trill

than: (or:

a) These thirds can be brought out with perfect distinctness only by means of this fingering, troublesome though it be.

b) It is self-evident that a hammering-out of these "passionate" eighth-notes in strict time would be incorrect in an aesthetic sense. By playing the first half of the measure with stronger emphasis (and hence greater freedom), as is demanded in particular by the peculiar rhythmic importance of the second eighth-note, and somewhat accelerating the second half, both the unity of the measure as such, and also the psychical agitation, receive due consideration. c) This melodic phrase, whose performance demands the intensest feeling, is probably to be understood thus: i.e., more singingly sustained than the marking denotes.

a) The literal execution is:

b) The repetition prescribed here according to custom impresses us as a chilling tautology.

c) This movement-figure, like the similar one in the right hand 4 measures further on, must be played entirely without accentuation; only in the principal modulations, e. g., the transition from F♯-minor to G-major and back, individual characteristic intervals may be slightly emphasized. On the other hand, a transformation of the figures into an indistinct *tremolo* would, of course, be wholly out of place.

155

a) In the analogous passage in the first division, this period embraces 4 measures, whereas it has but 3 here. There is no reason why either should be altered for the sake of symmetry of pattern. Both are good, and greater brevity and conciseness in form are æsthetically justified in repetitions.

a) This second hold (*pause*) may be sustained longer than the preceding. Further, a slight rest must intervene (for acoustic reasons, apart from esthetic ones) before the reëntrance of the first subject, as is indicated by a ⌢ over the bar.

a) There is no irreverence, even to the letter of the composer's work, in enhancing – in analogy with the D-minor Sonata, Op. 31, № 2 – the accent marked on the fourth beat by a chord struck with the left hand.

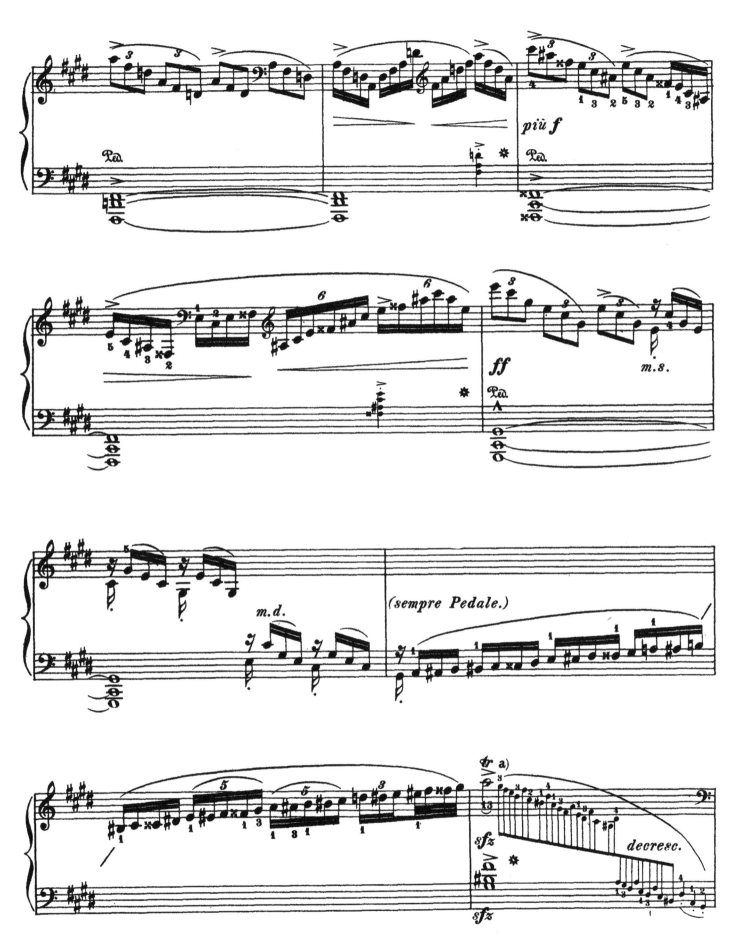

a) The Editor performs this cadenza with the following rhythmic divisions, the required *ritardando* then resulting as a matter of course:

159

a) *Adagio:* twice as slow as the *Presto*-movement, but not slower.

b) Avoid a *crescendo* in the preceding measures; the *forte* must enter with instantaneous abruptness, giving us a reproduction of the principal divisions in miniature— the deep melancholy of the *Adagio*, the wild desperation of the *Finale*.

SONATA.

Op. 26.

To Prince CARL von LICHNOWSKY.

Abbreviations: M. T. signifies Main Theme; S. T., Sub-Theme; Tr., Transition, R., Return.

Andante con Variazioni. (♩=80.)   L. van BEETHOVEN.

a) This arpeggio-mark is not found in the original; indeed, the Master employed it far more seldom than his predecessors Haydn and Mozart. Isolated exceptions (e. g., in Op. 7, Op. 31 № 2, etc.) simply confirm the easy conjecture, that the arpeggio style of playing was incompatible with his orchestral habit of thinking. Nevertheless, a moderately free use of the arpeggio in this place — and in various others as well — is eminently proper, not only on technical, but still more on acoustical, grounds (for the sake of euphony). The reproach of irreverence is disarmed by pointing to movements 1 and 2 of Op. 109, where we meet with a notation of chords in the form of small tied notes; — in Op. 27 № 2, Finale in C♯-minor, he even definitely indicates the breaking of the chord by rhythmically dividing it. An almost unnoticeable dwelling on the (melodically) most important highest tone is advisable, so as not to alter its relative value to the next. To be played nearly thus: and similarly in meas. 24:

b) The counter-melody in the left hand must be brought out in the same independent relief as the thematic song in the right, and with opposed shading.

c) Here the trill should undoubtedly be rounded off with an after-beat: although the Master desires this only where he expressly writes it (for instance, even in the initial theme of the Sonata with Violin, Op. 96, no after beat must be added).

Var. I.
Un poco più mosso. (♪ = 88.)

a) This taking of the lower tone of the octave with the left hand, in order to facilitate the *legato* in the melody, is equally applicable to the last eighth-note of the preceding measure.

b) In so-called bravura variations, intended to exhibit an applause-craving virtuosity, a pause after the theme, and between the several variations, is justifiable; but the art-form of the Variation, Beethoven's own peculiar creation, will not bear such a chilling interruption. The player should rather strive to attain flowing continuity, and to render the transitions (for instance, the acceleration in the tempo which is indispensable to the Third Variation, to prevent any effect of dragging) as imperceptible as possible.

Var. II.

Più animato, ma non troppo. (♪ = 96.)

a) The melody contained in the after-striking sixteenth-notes, while making itself felt throughout, must be played no louder (though a trifle *more firmly*, as indicated by the short dash ‿) than the anticipating bass notes alternating with them. Do not neglect to give due weight to the middle parts in the right hand, which are so essential as an harmonic filling.

b) A slight delay on the second eighth ‿ a momentary pause, as if at a semicolon ‿ is needful to introduce the remoter key (F-major) in which the middle section begins. This nuance may also be observed both in the Theme and the other Variations, although less imperatively demanded in these cases by euphonic considerations.

a) The *crescendo* in this retrogressional measure is borrowed from the original transition in the Theme, the shading and expression of which must be studiously followed in the performance of each Variation.

b) Observe the accompanying middle part in this and the next measure:

Var. III. (Minore.)
Più sostenuto. (♪ = 80.)

a) A signature of seven flats is unnecessary, and confuses the pupil's eye. Hummel, in his E♭ - minor quintet, was also content with the signature of the major key.

b) The sforzato - sign *sf* always applies only to the note or chord over or under which it stands——a rule carefully to be observed throughout this Variation and the next - following.

Var. IV.
Con moto. ($\quad$ = 92)

a) The dialogue-form characteristic of this Variation (whose mode of presentation, more especially the alternation between different registers, has often been imitated, particularly by Mendelssohn) requires, in our opinion, a corresponding characteristic shading, for which, especially in the middle section, we have marked a free mode of execution, easily modifiable according to individual taste. In the *sforzatos* themselves (meas. 20-25) certain gradations must be observed, as *sf = f, sf = mf, sf = p*,— in short, one should attempt to "color," but without interfering with the requirement of fluent execution (with sharp contrasts of *legato* and *staccato* in the two hands).

b) The normal fingering for *staccato* passages in thirds is elsewhere $\frac{4}{2}$ and $\frac{3}{1}$, the latter on white keys.

a) Not only the bass notes, but also the harmonic middle parts (as the first note in the right hand), may be held down: this is, indeed, indispensable for the production of the pianistic euphony evidently aimed at here by the composer.

b) Here the executant should remember the counter-melody for the right hand in the Theme:

a) This charming Coda must end dreamily, as if lost in reverie, but not begin so; therefore, no perceptible change in the Tempo should be made, letting the *calando,* both as regards tone-power and movement, creep on very gradually.

b) Some new editions have the unjustifiable alteration:

c) A strict *legato,* and not, as in the measure preceding and following, ...

d) The shading *pp* ⎯< ⎯> *pp* marked in some new editions is incorrect.

II. Scherzo.
Allegro molto. (♩.=88.)

a) The player should resist any inclination to retard; the more so, as these twelve measures before the reprise of the Theme are to be regarded, in themselves, as a *ritardando* of ample length.

b) It is quite as absurd to forbid the use of the thumb on black keys, as to forbid the substitution of a longer finger for this, the shortest of all, when thereby an unnecessary change in the position of the hand could be obviated, in deference to any pedantic system of fingering. In fact, every Beethoven player ought to prepare himself for any emergency — extraordinary demands on his technique — by diligently practising the scales in the flat keys with the fingering for C-major, a plan first suggested by Bertini.

Trio (l'istesso tempo.)

a) A brief pause before the reëntrance of the Scherzo would be entirely in keeping with a humoristic conception of these four genuinely Beethovenish transitional measures. They ought then to be played rather emphatically, as if angrily dismissing the trio-theme, and the reprise of the scherzo-theme taken up in a graceful, bantering style.

III. Marcia funebre sulla morte d'un eroe.
Andante maestoso.(♩=72.)

a) In contrast with most of the Master's sonatas, in which the internal psychological connection between the several movements is so marked that their regular succession cannot be interrupted without injury to the effect, this succession is entirely optional in Op. 26. In this particular it might well be called a (modernized) "Suite," no other unity besides that of key being apparent amid the rich and charming variety of its construction. For this reason, its four numbers may either be played each by itself, or in a different succession,—e.g., Dead March, Scherzo, Variations, Rondo, which might possibly be "more effective."

b) The lowest part in the right hand should be quitted to make way for the left on the third quarter, and similarly 4 and 8 measures further on.

c) Take care not to treat the two 16th-notes like the after-beat of a trill; they must be played thus:

a) The change of fingers marked here facilitates the *crescendo* in the tremolo, which must keep strictly to the given number of notes and strive after the effect of a military roll on the drums; in fact, this whole movement is conceived in a distinctly orchestral spirit, and should therefore be felt and colored in its reproduction like an orchestral piece.

a) This coda must by no means be treated like a "Bagatelle". Both the ascending and descending passages contain the sum, so to speak, of all agonizing woes, concentrated to wellnigh convulsive expression; and in spite of the modulation to major are not to be conceived as a reconciliation— as if their spirit justified an immediate passage to the lively Finale-Impromptu.

IV. Rondo.

Allegro. ($\bullet = 116$.)

M.T.

a) Here the Theme proper lies in the lower part; hence the left hand must play somewhat louder than the right, which, though playing the same tones, reverses their order, whereby their melodious connection is dissolved, and their significance reduced to that of a mere figurate accompaniment.

b) Though extremely few expression-marks occur in the original, the material invites so great a variety of shading that we have felt justified in making numerous additions in this regard, in order to prevent the player from falling into an indiscriminating "reading-off" or "rattling-off," such as many self-appointed guardians of the classics still unhappily declare to be canonical.

a) The marking as a sextuplet in the original is doubtless an oversight, and likewise contradicts the twice-repeated marking as a double triplet in analogous passages (20 and 18 measures before the close). A $\widehat{6}$ over sixteenth-notes indicates one triplet of eighths, not two of sixteenths.

a) Variety is the spice of life. For the repetition of the first subject we have proposed a shading different from that first employed; the player may adopt whichever he pleases. The main point is, in any event, *to shade* -- to lend life, animation and movement to the performance. The omission of expression-marks on the composer's part is to be regarded simply as a permission for individual freedom of interpretation.

a) This C-minor Episode may be compared, in its character and in the energetic manner of expression suited to it, with the A-minor Episode in the Rondo of Op. 53, or (to quote an example in grander style) with the G-minor Episode in the Finale of the Sinfonia eroica. The fingering, approved by experience, though it may appear peculiar at a first reading, is more reliable than the 3 1 4 1 4 2 after the Clementi-Hummel method, which latter is wanting in regularly recurring points of support.

b) The fingering for passages in broken thirds in *legato* may also be copied from that for simultaneous thirds in *staccato* (comp. Note b on Page 221); thus: 4 2 4 1 4 2 4 1, etc.

a) In *staccato* octave-passages it is best to use the fifth finger instead of the fourth on the black keys
as well, to secure uniformity in the position of the hand (and also in the actual down-stroke).

a) To get the *sforzato* effect, which should be strongly marked, a break is necessary, i.e., the finger concerned must be lifted independently.

b) It is needless to say how un-Beethovenish it would be to couple the *diminuendo* with the slightest *ritardando*. Even an acceleration of the closing measures would be more allowable.